A souvenir guide

Women and Power: The Struggle for Suffrage

Sophie Duncan and Rachael Lennon

1909

❋ National Trust

Women and Power at the National Trust

This year marks the centenary of the 1918 Representation of the People Act which gave the vote to women over the age of 30 who were householders or married to householders. It was a milestone in the long history of the struggle for female suffrage.

The extraordinary historical breadth and geographical reach of National Trust properties allows us to explore fundamental events and movements in our nation's history. The lives of women are woven into the fabric of our places. This book tells the story of those who took the fight for female suffrage into the public arena in the face of violent opposition. Women across the social spectrum – from artists, writers and society hostesses to factory workers and kitchenmaids – became ardent campaigners for the movement.

When we cast our vote at the ballot box today with our minds full of the political realities of the moment, we perhaps don't always consider the bravery of those who fought for one of our most important rights: engagement in the political processes that govern our lives.

We are delighted to celebrate this important anniversary with you, as part of our **Women and Power** programme of exhibitions and events exploring the histories of women from across Trust properties in England, Wales and Northern Ireland.

Tarnya Cooper, Curatorial and Collections Director

Suffragettes demonstrate in a London street, 1912

Foreword by Everyday Sexism founder Laura Bates

In early 2012, a man followed me home, aggressively propositioning me and refusing to take no for an answer. Later that week, another man groped me on the bus, and a few days later two men in the street made graphic comments about my body. Had the incidents not happened so closely together, I never would have thought twice about any of them. They were simply part of being a woman.

I started the Everyday Sexism Project the same year to collect testimonies of harassment, discrimination and abuse from women around the world, aiming to raise awareness of the scale of the problem. I was shocked by the sheer amount of resistance to the simple notion of gender equality. Like many feminist activists before me, I was threatened, ridiculed and abused by people who wanted to silence me. One thing that sustained me was the stories of those who had gone before me, fighting for change, battling on against resistance.

The National Trust's Women and Power programme offers a precious opportunity to feel a close connection to such women through the places in which they lived. Places like Bodnant Garden, Conwy, home to generations of women who didn't give up fighting for what they believed in, and Killerton, Devon, where conflict raged in the Acland family between suffragist and anti-suffragist generations. In particular, I think of those ordinary women, not remembered on plaques or recorded in the history books, who poured everything into the struggle for women's equality, never to be memorialised or thanked. Women like Violet Ann Bland, a kitchenmaid at Dudmaston Hall, Shropshire, who would go on to become a passionate suffragette and endure force-feeding. To visit these places and understand such stories is to relive a battle for equality that continues to this day.

It took years of campaigning and direct action by law-abiding suffragists, and even violence and hunger strikes by the militant suffragettes, to achieve the Representation of the People Act of 1918. It would be another decade before all women gained the same voting rights as men.

In the ensuing 100 years, huge strides have been made towards gender equality in Britain, but there's still a way to go. An estimated 54,000 women lose their jobs every year as a result of maternity discrimination, and an average of two women are killed by a current or former partner every week. Fewer than one-third of our MPs are women, and there are more than three times as many men named John running FTSE 100 companies as all the female CEOs combined.

Playwright George Bernard Shaw, who joined suffrage marches and donated to the cause, said: 'The vote will never be won by speeches made by men on behalf of women… The speaking must be done by the women themselves.' His words are a powerful reminder that the stories and voices of those who have gone before us remain as important as ever.

Laura Bates is the founder of the Everyday Sexism Project and author of Everyday Sexism *and* Girl Up.

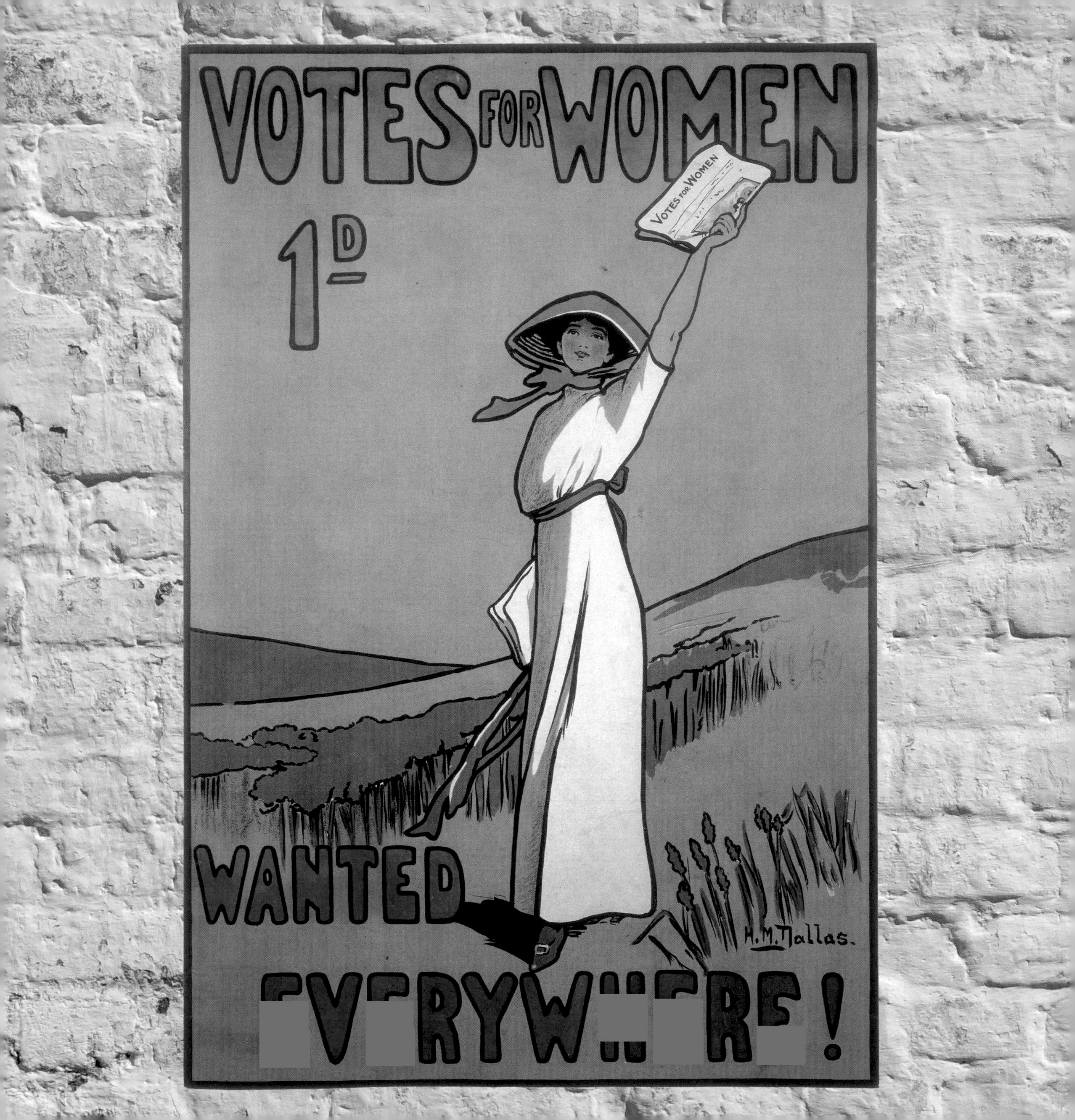
VOTES FOR WOMEN
1D
VOTES FOR WOMEN
WANTED
H.M. Dallas.

The Struggle for Suffrage

The struggle for suffrage raged across decades and generations. It was argued in press and Parliament, fought in the nation's streets and reached the most intimate spheres of people's lives.

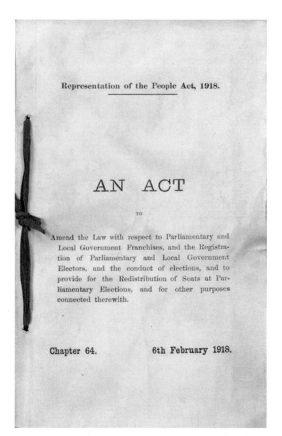

A century after the Representation of the People Act of 1918, this guidebook reveals the debates heard in the drawing rooms, kitchens and bedrooms of National Trust places as the country decided whether women might have a voice in public life. We continue to see the footprints of this intensely personal political argument in the houses and collections cared for by the Trust.

Women who sought to exercise their voice through a ballot box found themselves faced with an entrenched opposition. In 1897, near her home at **Wallington**, in Northumberland, Caroline Philips reflected: 'Monopoly and privilege are naturally the portion of the strong and the powerful, and these privileges always die hard.' Across generations, both men and women passionately fought to prevent the political equality of women.

In 2018, the National Trust is marking the centenary of women's suffrage with a series of exhibitions, events, artist commissions and podcasts. We will use this foundation to take a step forward in redressing the wider representation of women's voices in the history of England, Wales and Northern Ireland.

Women and Power is part of the National Trust's Challenging Histories series. Building on Prejudice and Pride in 2017, we will continue to reveal hidden histories across our places and explore a fuller picture of our shared past for generations to come.

Opposite 1909 poster advertising the *Votes for Women* newspaper, designed by Women's Social and Political Union (WSPU) member Hilda Dallas. Dallas studied at the Slade School of Art and used the iconic suffragette colours of green, purple and white in many of her designs

Left The Representation of the People Act 1918

Timeline

1867

The **National Society for Women's Suffrage** is formed.

1868

First ever public meeting on women's suffrage is held in Manchester, with speakers including Agnes Pochin of **Bodnant**.

1897

The **National Union of Women's Suffrage Societies** (NUWSS) forms, supported by over 20 societies, and led by Millicent Fawcett.

1902

A delegation of northern women textile workers presents a 37,000-strong petition to Parliament, demanding the vote.

1905

Militancy begins. Christabel Pankhurst and Annie Kenney are arrested and imprisoned for interrupting a meeting of the Liberal Party. The slogans 'Deeds Not Words' and 'Votes for Women' emerge.

1907

The **Qualification of Women Act** allows women to be elected to borough and county councils, and as mayors.

1883

Alice Acland of **Killerton** co-founds the **Co-operative Women's Guild**.

1881

The Isle of Man grants vote to women.

1903

Manchester suffragist Emmeline Pankhurst breaks from the NUWSS to form the **Women's Social and Political Union (WSPU)** with her daughters Christabel and Sylvia.

1888

Local Government Act allows women to vote at elections in county and borough councils.

1908

Up to 500,000 activists attend mass rally in Hyde Park. Non-response from PM Asquith leads to suffragettes smashing Downing Street windows and tying themselves to railings. The **Actresses' Franchise League** is formed, with founder members Ellen Terry, Edith Craig and Lillie Langtry. **Women's National Anti-Suffrage League** forms.

1866

John Stuart Mill MP presents a petition for women's suffrage to the House of Commons. It fails. Suffrage societies start in Edinburgh, London and Manchester.

1912

The **Parliamentary Franchise (Women) Bill** is defeated by 222 votes to 208. Suffragettes respond with a mass window-smashing campaign.

1914

Suffrage prisoners set free to join the war effort; campaigning suspended.

1928

Amendment of the Representation of the People Act allows everyone over the age of 21 to vote.

1909

The **Men's National Anti-Suffrage League** forms. Liberals introduce a radical Suffrage Bill, which is delayed by economic disputes and stalled by a General Election. The beginning of force-feeding.

1918

The **Representation of the People Act** is passed, giving the vote to all men over 30, and women over 30 who were householders or married to householders, owners of property worth more than £5, or university graduates.

1910

Asquith fails to pass the Conciliation Bill. **'Black Friday'** protest by the WSPU: some suffragettes are permanently or fatally (in the long term) injured. Sexual abuse by police. The **National League for Opposing Women's Suffrage** forms from a merger of the men and women's societies.

1913

There are now 46 suffrage groups in the UK and Ireland. Bomb and arson campaigns; increasing arrests; the **'Cat and Mouse' Act**. **Emily Wilding Davison** steps in front of the King's horse at the Derby and dies four days later.

THE DERBY TRAGEDY : AT TATTENHAM CORNER
A SUFFRAGETTE'S MAD RUSH AND ITS CONSEQUENCES

1923

Matrimonial Causes Act makes grounds for divorce the same for men and women.

1922

Law of Property Act allows husband and wife equal inheritance rights.

1919

Nancy Astor of **Cliveden** becomes the first female MP to take up her seat in the House of Commons.

Spheres of Influence

Over the course of the 19th century, women's role in society – and what it meant to be a woman – began to be questioned.

Throughout the 19th century, the lives of the women who lived and worked in places now looked after by the National Trust were strictly defined and confined by their sex. Until the 1870s, women could not access university education, and until 1882 could not own property after marriage. From 1864, under the Contagious Diseases Acts any woman could be arrested, gynaecologically examined and imprisoned if police suspected she was a prostitute – simply because she had been seen talking to a sailor. A husband could divorce his wife solely for adultery, whereas until 1937 she had to prove cruelty, incest or sodomy on his part. Rape did not count as cruelty: under marriage laws not repealed until 1991, a wife was believed to have irrevocably consented to sex with her husband.

'We are constantly reminded of women assuming the functions of men.'

Hampshire Advertiser (1889)

Victorian press. The New Woman's penchant for horrifyingly unfeminine pastimes (Smoking! Bicycling! *Tennis!*) seemed bound to lead not only to the collapse of civilisation but – as the *Hampshire Advertiser* warned in 1889 – to 'the sprouting of hairs upon the upper lip' as the consequence of 'assuming the functions of men'. To conform was feminine; to rebel would masculinise women, and nothing could be worse.

Above all, the Victorian era pilloried women who were different, whether on grounds of class, sexuality, ability or race. Rebels had to be crushed. Thus, Martha Solomon, the black South African Countess of Stamford and her daughter Lady Mary Grey could be mocked as a 'Hottentot countess and her dusky daughter', when the Countess dared to fight for her mixed-race son's right to inherit his father's title and lands at **Dunham Massey**.

As Bill Drummond MP put it in 1857, the House of Commons was 'a court of men judging women according to their own estimate and for their own purpose'. Without the vote, women had no opportunity to participate in democracy to improve their lives. Population imbalances between women and men created 'superfluous women' in British society from the 1850s onwards, with the 1851 census recording nearly 2.5 million spinsters or widows. But women's lives were changing, and Victorian Britain saw a gathering force of debate around what became 'The Woman Question': what did it mean to be a woman?

The New Woman
With the first women's colleges at Cambridge (1869) and Oxford (1879) came the stereotype of the 'New Woman'. Educated and independent, with a worrying indifference to marriage, the New Woman was swiftly vilified by the late-

Ideals of womanhood

Victorian and Edwardian arguments against suffrage clearly reveal the ideal that women were meant to fulfil: a domestic angel who exercised her moral influence over husband and family, and who clung to the private sphere.

Even when benevolent impulses led women to charitable work, National Trust founder Octavia Hill (1838–1912) cautioned that women should confine themselves to 'silent, out-of-sight work'. Writing to *The Times* in 1910 to declare her opposition to suffrage, she exhorted woman to concentrate on 'her duties, not on her rights […] let her seek to do her own work steadily and earnestly, looking rather to the out-of-sight, neglected sphere'. Feminist author George Eliot (1819–1880) ended her most famous novel, *Middlemarch*, with the reflection that most women improved the world through 'unhistoric acts', and 'lived faithfully a hidden life, and rest in unvisited tombs'.

Simultaneously, scientific and medical advances debated women's health. The late 19th century saw the advent of modern psychiatry and gynaecology. Some medics felt that education damaged women's nervous and reproductive systems, with biologist Herbert Spencer blaming 'merciless application' for the abundance of 'pale, angular' young women. Conversely, the politically radical, anti-eugenicist Horatio Bryan Donkin attributed an apparent epidemic of *fin-de-siècle* female hysteria and depression to women's restrictive lives: the '"Thou shalt not" that meets a girl at every turn'.

Octavia Hill's 1910 letter to *The Times* reflected the Established Church's values: a woman who kept to the 'out-of-sight, neglected sphere' was 'filling the place to which by God's appointment she is called'. The political establishment was equally clear on what women owed to society. As Winston Churchill wrote in 1897, women should 'discharge their duty to the state, viz marrying and giving birth to children'. Lord Curzon of **Kedleston**, Britain's leading male anti-suffragist, expanded this further: women's suffrage would 'be an injury [...] to the great organisations to which both sexes belong, namely, the State and the Empire'.

Women against suffrage

Apart from Hill, many of Britain's most powerful female philanthropists were anti-suffrage. Women including Gertrude Acland, chatelaine of **Killerton**, and Henrietta, Duchess of Newcastle, at **Clumber Park**, worked successfully for the church, and with charities for improving the welfare of women and children – but felt they had no need of the vote. They deemed their political views adequately represented by their husbands – or, in the case of Adelaide Watt at **Speke Hall**, by their male tenants' votes, which she sought to direct. This only worked for women in happy marriages, or privileged women with other kinds of political influence or power.

It perhaps explains why influential women such as Beatrix Potter (1866–1943) and Florence Nightingale (1820–1910) felt, as the latter put it, that 'in the years that I have passed in government offices, I have never felt the want of a vote'. Working-class women, meanwhile, remained voiceless, in workplaces characterised by unequal pay and sexual exploitation.

Opposite Social reformer and National Trust founder Octavia Hill, painted by John Singer Sargent, 1898

Above (left) Pioneer of modern nursing, Florence Nightingale

Above (right) Artist, writer and farmer Beatrix Potter, standing at her Hill Top porch

Professional pioneers

Some women, however, did develop successful and independent careers, especially in academia and the arts.

Caroline Augusta Foley (1857–1942), granddaughter of the family at **Felbrigg**, was both a suffrage campaigner and a pioneering scholar of Pali and Buddhism. Agnes Garrett (1845–1935), sister of leading suffragists Millicent Fawcett and Elizabeth Garrett Anderson, established with her cousin Rhoda Garrett the first all-female interior decorators' company, 'R & A Garrett', exhibiting in London and Paris. Today, their furniture can still be seen at **Standen**. Rhoda in particular was a star speaker, arguing in 1872 that the vote would allow women 'to look after their own interests'.

Actress Dame Ellen Terry (1847–1928) of **Smallhythe** became Britain's highest-paid woman after Queen Victoria. Terry's eloquence and professional volition embodied the freedom suffragists craved. She became an activist's role model, reinterpreting Shakespeare's heroines as 'having more in common with our modern revolutionaries' in lectures to suffrage societies, and modelling public speaking for a generation of women learning to use their own voices.

Terry's daughter, the actress, producer and designer Edith Craig (1869–1947), 'grew up quite firmly certain that no self-respecting woman could be other than a Suffragist'. Craig sold the *Votes for Women* newspaper and helped devise *A Pageant of Great Women* alongside Cicely Hamilton. The *Pageant* showcased historical heroines including Sappho, Joan of Arc and Florence Nightingale. At its climax, the character 'Woman' addressed men everywhere: 'I stand/For the clear right to hold my life my own' and 'This you must know:/The world is mine, as yours.'

Lillah McCarthy, a suffragette actress, personally inspired Emmeline Pankhurst, while a single speech by actress Elizabeth Robins transformed Evelyn Sharp into a suffragette. Robins was a stunningly beautiful, controversial playwright and performer. As Sharp wrote, 'From that moment I was not to know again for twelve years, if indeed ever again, what it meant to cease from mental strife.' She joined the Women's Social and Political Union (WSPU), becoming a militant suffragette who was imprisoned for her activism.

Opposite (left) Lillah McCarthy, suffragette actress and inspiration to Emmeline Pankhurst, photographed by George Bernard Shaw

Opposite (right) The iconic Ellen Terry, photographed as Lady Macbeth

Right Terry painted in the same role by John Singer Sargent in 1889

Below Suffragette composer Dame Ethel Smyth, 1927. Smyth composed the anthem of the suffrage movement, The March of the Women, and served time in Royal Holloway prison for window smashing

George Bernard Shaw (1856–1950) of **Shaw's Corner** was the theatre's most famous pro-suffrage playwright. In his (banned) play *Mrs Warren's Profession*, he argued that conventional Victorian marriage constituted legalised prostitution. Famously garrulous, Shaw nevertheless refused to speak at suffrage demonstrations, explaining: 'Every time you ask a man to appear on your platform, you consent the insufficiency of women to plead their cause.'

'Thinking is my fighting'

The 20th century's most famous feminist writer, Virginia Woolf, took an inconsistent role in the suffrage movement. Although biographers have tended to downplay her involvement with The National Union of Women's Suffrage Societies (NUWSS) in 1910, she remained with them for several months, her activism curtailed by an outbreak of the mental illness that plagued her. Woolf was later proud of having 'worked for the vote', as she told Benedict Nicolson, son of Vita Sackville-West, while living at **Monk's House**. Although close to suffragists like Ray Strachey and, later, former suffragette composer Ethel Smyth, Woolf's longest-term association was with the radical Co-operative Women's Guild.

The Guild, founded by Alice Acland, **Killerton**'s suffragist mistress, aimed to improve women's lives, via suffrage, health education and professional benefits including maternity leave. It shared Alice's belief, articulated in 1883, that 'England can never be all it might, when more than one-half of the nation hangs behind the other half.'

Like many staunch supporters of women's rights, Woolf stopped short of actual militancy throughout her long association with the Co-operative and, later, the Anti-Fascist movement in Britain. Her writing was, for her, a form of activism, as she wrote in 1936 contemplating fascism's rise: 'What can I do but write?' and, in 1940, 'Thinking is my fighting'.

Emily Wilding Davison

One woman who became central to the suffragette story was Emily Wilding Davison (1872–1913) (see pages 40–41). After careers as a teacher and governess, she found true fulfilment in suffrage, writing to the *Votes for Women* newspaper in 1909 that being a suffragette gave her 'a fullness of job and an interest in living which I never before experienced'.

Above Virginia Woolf's outdoor writing room at Monk's House with (left to right) Angelica Garnett (née Bell), Vanessa and Clive Bell, Virginia Woolf and John Maynard Keynes

'The very salt of life'

Towards the end of the 19th century, Victorian cities' geography started changing in ways that offered some women more freedom. Department stores, women-only clubs and 'Dorothy' restaurants allowed affluent women to shop and meet unchaperoned, spend more time out of the house, and to have credit accounts in their own names, not their husband's.

Nevertheless, even for many privileged women, life had changed little since the suffragist Agnes Pochin (née Heap), later co-owner of **Bodnant**, wrote in 1855 that 'Woman's life […] is, and has been rendered, essentially a dull one.' The result was that suffrage activism became, as Margaret, Lady Rhondda (who donated **Sugarloaf Mountain** to the Trust), remembered, 'the very salt of life. The knowledge of it had come like a draught of fresh air into our padded, stifled lives.'

Politics

The late Victorian and Edwardian eras saw oscillations between Liberal and Tory governments. The last years of Queen Victoria were filled with uncertainty about the succession: her heir, Edward VII, was ageing, dissolute and a notorious womaniser. Anti-Semitic figures in the British establishment also objected to his close friendships with prominent Jews, including his financial adviser, Sir Ernest Cassel. Conservative commentators saw the decadence of the *fin de siècle* as a sign of Britain's degeneration.

Regardless of who was in government, two issues besides women's suffrage dominated politics: Home Rule in Ireland and the Second Boer War (1899–1902). Suffragist women were active in campaigning on both issues. The South African suffragist Elizabeth Maria Molteno (1852–1927), who is buried in the Trevone churchyard on the National Trust's **Trevose Head Heritage Coast**, campaigned against the British concentration camps housing Boer War prisoners in South Africa.

In many ways, however, the story of the suffrage campaign is the story of the Liberal Party. Herbert Henry Asquith, Liberal Prime Minister from 1908–1916, was personally very anti-suffrage. Liberal women who had agitated for the vote while retaining party loyalties felt increasingly let down. By 1893, suffragist Annie

Right *Fabian Essays*, edited and published by suffrage supporter George Bernard Shaw, 1889

Leigh Browne, who donated land in **The Byes, Sidmouth** to the National Trust, told the *Woman's Herald*: 'I am tired of being told to wait patiently and help the Liberal Party, seeing that it is 25 years since I attended for the first time a Woman's Suffrage meeting.'

Class privilege apparently united elite politicians, who socialised across party divides: Asquith regularly dined and stayed at **Cliveden**, as the guest of Tory MP Waldorf Astor and his wife, the future MP Nancy Astor. However, working-class political movements were forming. George Bernard Shaw helped to write the Fabian Society's first manifesto (1884) which demanded equal suffrage. He and his wife Charlotte Payne-Townshend were close friends with the writer and suffragette Eleanor Marx Aveling, daughter of Karl Marx. Emmeline Pankhurst and her husband Richard were also Fabians, as was universal suffragist Susan Lawrence, who later lived at **Buscot Park**. In 1906, Keir Hardie became the first leader of the newly christened Labour Party, which from its outset campaigned for women's suffrage, and from 1907 for universal suffrage.

Left Watercolour of Prime Minister Herbert Henry Asquith by Sir Leslie Ward, published in *Vanity Fair*, 1904

Below The Labour Group in the House of Commons, 1906

'I am tired of being told to wait patiently and help the Liberal Party.'

Annie Leigh Browne, Liberal suffragist (1893)

COPYRIGHT   THE LABOUR GROUP IN THE HOUSE OF COMMONS, PHOTOGRAPHED FEB. 13th 1906 ON THE TERRACE   (PHOTO PARK)

Political wives

A number of suffragists began as politicians' wives. Political wives were expected to offer active and decorative support to their husbands' careers through canvassing, speeches and entertaining influential allies. Many women fulfilled this role – Nancy Astor recalled that she 'must have knocked on thirty thousand doors' for husband Waldorf. Molly Trevelyan, the suffragist wife of Liberal MP Sir Charles Trevelyan, owner of **Wallington**, breastfed her baby between meetings, while canvassing in January 1906.

Other couples diverged politically. Winston Churchill wrote in 1897 that suffrage was 'contrary to natural law'. His future wife, Clementine Hozier (1885–1977) disagreed, and the two clashed as a married couple at **Chartwell**.

In 1909, Winston , who had suffered threats and assaults from suffragettes, told Clementine that he could not support their militancy: 'I shall never try to crush your convictions [but] I must claim an equal liberty for myself.' Clementine's 'equal liberty' included writing a satirical letter to *The Times* in 1912. After bacteriologist Almroth Wright argued that women's physiological inadequacy barred them from political life, Clementine sarcastically inquired whether women shouldn't be banned altogether. Her letter parodied misogynist perceptions of progressive women as hysterical frumps: 'If they take up a profession, the indelicacy of their minds makes them undesirable partners [...] if not quite insane, many of them have to be shut up.' Scathingly begging Wright to 'crown his many achievements by delivering mankind from the parasitic, demented, and immoral species,' she signed herself 'One of the Doomed'.

Left Edith Vane-Tempest-Stewart, painted in evening wear by Philip de László in 1927

Some wives were uninterested in sharing the political limelight – at least before suffrage. After Charles Vane-Tempest-Stewart became a Unionist MP in 1906, his wife Edith (1878–1959) was highly averse to campaigning at **Mount Stewart** in Northern Ireland. Suffrage, not wifely duty, radicalised her. Edith became an ardent suffragist and a highly popular speaker and writer. Her pamphlet, 'Women's Direct Influence', deconstructed the Lady Macbeth-like role of a supportive Edwardian wife: 'How often do we hear that "so and so" owes his position politically to a great extent through the agency of a clever wife; and we know that the essential feature of her cleverness consists in disguising its existence from her husband, and only so by doing can she obtain what she is striving for, either for him or for herself.' For the first time, suffrage campaign allowed women to use their talents to improve their own civil rights.

'Nothing except the cause of Woman Suffrage could have launched me off as a platform speaker.'

Edith Vane-Tempest-Stewart

Right Lady Nancy Astor, painted by John Singer Sargent in 1908

Risking a Change
1868–1905

'Women have been greatly neglected,
physically and educationally.'
Sarah Grand (1894)

Families united

Many families living and working in National Trust places found themselves united at home in the fight to achieve votes for women. For the most privileged families, the necessity for political franchise might be less immediate. Women with alternative means of accessing power, and women who thrived in the status quo, did not necessarily feel any desire to see political change. This saw some families united in their open opposition to women's votes.

In 1889, over 100 women (most of them titled) signed an Appeal Against Female Suffrage declaring that the enfranchisement of women would be a 'national calamity' and 'a total misconception of women's true dignity and special mission'. The published petition rejected any need for Victorian women to access the vote when, 'during the past half century, all the principal injustices of the law towards women have been amended.'

Lady Randolph Churchill was amongst the signatories and, in 1897, her son Winston, of **Chartwell** in Kent, highlighted the role of class in the debates as he claimed that 'only the most undesirable class of women are eager for the right.' For other politically active families, united towards progressive change, the cause of votes for women could become part of an ongoing and shared activism.

Industrial radicals

At **Wightwick**, near Wolverhampton, numerous members of the Mander family were active Liberals and radicals connected with the suffrage movement. In the late 19th and early 20th centuries, Wolverhampton was a hub of industry and radical politics. A number of notable activists spoke in the city and were visited, or even hosted, by the Mander family at Wightwick.

In January 1875, Samuel Small Mander chaired a meeting at St George's Hall in Wolverhampton at which Lydia Becker, leader in the early British

suffrage movement and founder of the *Women's Suffrage Journal*, was invited to speak. Geoffrey Mander and his first wife (Rosalind) Florence Caverhill were both members of the Wolverhampton Women's Suffrage Society and were regularly joined by Millicent Fawcett.

The Manders sought to model their progressive ideology within their household, supporting opportunities for their employees. In 1900, Emma Smith, the housekeeper at Wightwick, and her governess friend Miss Fielding attended a lecture by prominent suffragist Sarah Grand. Grand had coined the term 'New Woman' in 1894 and defended her radical politics to the Wolverhampton audience, observing: 'It has been said that women are drifting away from the hearth and the home… Women have been greatly neglected, physically and educationally.' Grand found a supportive audience and Smith later wrote to Flora Mander, whose tickets they had used, that both women had 'most thoroughly enjoyed' the lecture. In the correspondence carefully conserved at Wightwick, we can see a 19th-century network openly exploring gendered politics.

Opposite Sarah Grand, photographed with her bicycle in 1896. Grand had coined the term the 'New Woman' two years earlier

Above (left) Rosalind Florence Mander, widely known as Flora

Above (right) Geoffrey Mander in Royal Flying Corps uniform, 1918

Families united (continued)

At **Quarry Bank** in Cheshire, the Greg family shared a Unitarian faith, which provided a foundation for their political activities. The diary of Alice Dowson, daughter of pioneer factory owner Samuel Greg, brings to life frequent happy family gatherings at Quarry Bank House. The Gregs were cotton manufacturers and, though the conditions of the workers at Quarry Bank Mill were harsh, Dowson's diary speaks of a family campaigning for women's rights alongside causes such as care of the sick, an end to vivisection and the repeal of the Contagious Diseases Acts.

For Dowson, these campaigns were connected to the need for women to have a political voice; most particularly as she fought to end the state's moral judgement and violent treatment of vulnerable women and girls suspected of being prostitutes. She hosted meetings to oppose the Contagious Diseases Acts in her home, and in 1897 she attended a women's suffrage meeting to oppose the possibility of the introduction of the Acts in India.

Though disagreements arose, the Greg family seem to have navigated political difference well. We can see a fiery exception in a diary entry of 1879 when Dowson argues with a cousin: 'He and I got into a furious discussion about the laws for the sexes and I got so fierce the children were quite astonished.' Alice Dowson proudly continued her fight for women's rights alongside her 10 children and her husband, who also campaigned to raise the age of consent for girls to 16 in 1885. Her prominence grew in the 1900s and, after having chaired a suffrage meeting in 1908, she proudly recalled: 'All my five daughters were there!'

'Papa and I (and mother a little) and afterwards Ben, got into a tremendous talk and argument about women's rights questions and C.D. acts etc. […] which was very interesting and very good to have had. We ended very good friends.'

Diary of Alice Dowson (1871)

Right **Workers at Quarry Bank Mill in Cheshire**

Mothers and daughters

The debate was fought across decades and generations and called mothers and daughters to participate together. At **Smallhythe**, Ellen Terry and Edith Craig created a hub of liberal creative thinking. **Sugarloaf Mountain** in Wales was donated to the National Trust by suffragette Margaret Mackworth, later Viscountess Rhondda, who was active in the movement alongside her mother Sybil Thomas. At **Bodnant**, also in Wales, Agnes Pochin and her daughter Laura McLaren, were both leading national figures in publishing and speaking for women's right to vote.

Left Quarry Bank Mill, the Greg family's 18th-century cotton mill in Cheshire

Above Ellen Terry and her daughter Edith Craig, captured in an intimate moment

Families divided

Though some women entered the political arena alongside their families, or with their support, for others, their participation was more than family amity could sustain. The issue could become a wedge, pushing into existing cracks in family views on the world. Often, though by no means always, these lines of divide fell between generations.

We can find the relatives of many prominent activists and suffragists in the 1889 anti-women's suffrage petition. Julia Stephen, mother to artist Vanessa Bell and writer Virginia Woolf, signed the statement. From **Alderley Edge** in Cheshire, Henrietta Stanley added her name. Stanley's daughter, Katharine Russell, Viscountess Amberley, was an ardent suffragist who campaigned for birth control, used pioneer Elizabeth Garrett Anderson as her personal doctor, counted Emily Wilding Davison among her admirers and was president of the Bristol branch of the National Society for Women's Suffrage. On hearing that she had taken up this position in 1870, Queen Victoria wrote: 'I am most anxious to enlist everyone who can speak or write to join in checking this mad, wicked folly of "Women's Rights" […] Lady Amberley ought to get a good whipping.'

'A young hound running riot'
Theresa, Marchioness of Londonderry, on her suffragist daughter-in-law, Edith Vane-Tempest-Stewart

Left **Edith Vane-Tempest-Stewart painted with her favourite dog, Fly, by Philip de László, 1913**

Right **Portrait of suffrage campaigner Eleanor Acland by Florence Veric Hardy Small**

At **Mount Stewart** in Northern Ireland, Edith Vane-Tempest-Stewart was a passionate campaigner for women's votes. Both Edith's father and her mother-in-law disapproved. The latter was a traditional female philanthropist and, like fellow anti-suffrage campaigner Gertrude Acland, had participated in more ostensibly appropriate campaigns such as the promotion of the state registration of nurses. At **Killerton** in Exeter, Acland experienced her own family conflict on the issue of women's suffrage, with opinions divided across three generations. Acland was President of the Exeter Anti-Suffrage League and hosted an anti-suffrage garden party at Killerton in 1910. Her sister-in-law Alice Acland was a committed suffragist and mother-in-law to Eleanor Acland, founder of the Liberal Women's Suffrage Union. Each of these influential Acland women, and their husbands, fought their personal differences around women's right to vote on the public stage.

Uncharted arguments

The exposure of family differences cannot have been comfortable for anyone. These recorded, high-profile disagreements represent only a fraction of the family debates over this question held across the nation over decades. It is impossible to quantify the unrecorded tensions and domestic disputes that occurred in the nation's homes; arguments between parents and children, siblings, husbands and wives. For women, the domestic sphere has long been politicised and questions regarding the unequal rights of sons and daughters have, inevitably, been taken personally.

The movement before militancy

In 1871, the year after Queen Victoria recommended her 'a good whipping', Lady Amberley published a 'ten-point-plan' demanding 'that the franchise should be extended to women as a means of power and protection in all matters affected by legislative action'.

Votes for women sat alongside nine other steps towards tackling the profound and entrenched gender inequality of Victorian Britain. The article argued for: better school education for girls; equal access to university degrees; access to all professions; married women's property rights; widows' legal recognition as sole guardians of their children; equal access to political and social

advocated new ideas, and pressed forward changes in social life, would always find the undertaking hard, and sometimes discouraging, and their successes few and far between.'

As the movement towards women voting in Britain became increasingly coordinated, so too did its entrenched opposition. As the debate escalated, a step-change was coming, also to be born in northern England.

work; public opinion in favour of all occupations to women; an end to legal subordination in marriage; and equal pay for equal work. In 2018, her demands have still yet to be achieved.

Before those who sought votes for women resorted to violence, the question had been debated for seven decades; men and women had campaigned with some momentum for over 30 years. Petitions had been painstakingly compiled, arguments and pamphlets published, speeches made, and marches taken over parks and streets.

Agnes Pochin published *The Right of Women to Exercise the Elective Franchise* under the pseudonym 'Justitia' in 1855. In April 1868 she spoke at the first public suffrage meeting in the country at the Manchester Free Trade Hall. Chaired by her husband, the Mayor of Salford, the meeting was also attended by their daughter, Laura. Agnes was publically criticised for sitting on the platform and Laura's later publication, *Better and Happier,* gives a clear picture of challenging and challenged, monotonous activism.

In the North East, at **Wallington**, Caroline Philips experienced similar frustration as president of the Women's Liberal Associations of Northumberland and Durham. In 1897 she addressed a group in Morpeth: 'Those who

'How often have we tramped along the muddy lanes, how often have we gone round from door to door, often receiving rebuffs and unkindness. Well do we remember dreary railway stations at midnight, the last train gone, and snow upon the ground.'

Laura Pochin, *Better and Happier* (1908 pamphlet)

Above Women peacefully marching on a London road, promoting a suffrage meeting, 1912

Right A suffrage petition for Prime Minister Asquith is signed by two suffragists in 1912. Petitions played a predominant role in the campaign for votes for women

Deeds Not Words
1905–1913

In early 1905, with waning press interest in the suffrage campaign, militancy began. Over the next few years, direct action would increase to include window-breaking, stone-throwing and bombing.

The pro-violence Women's Social and Political Union (WSPU) was formed in 1903. Leaders Emmeline Pankhurst and her daughter Christabel had become increasingly impatient with the NUWSS's insistence on peaceful tactics. The first suffragettes to be arrested were Christabel Pankhurst and Annie Kenney, for heckling Sir Edward Grey at a London meeting in October 1905. The word 'suffragette' began to be used to describe the militant activists, first coined by the *Daily Mail* in January 1906.

Above A suffragette committee meeting, 1906, featuring (left to right) Christabel Pankhurst, Annie Kenney, Nellie Martel, Emmeline Pankhurst and Charlotte Despard (née French)

Right Emmeline Pankurst addresses a crowd in Trafalgar Square in 1908

'Window-breaking, when Englishmen do it, is regarded as honest expression of political opinion. Window-breaking, when Englishwomen do it, is treated as a crime.'

Emmeline Pankhurst

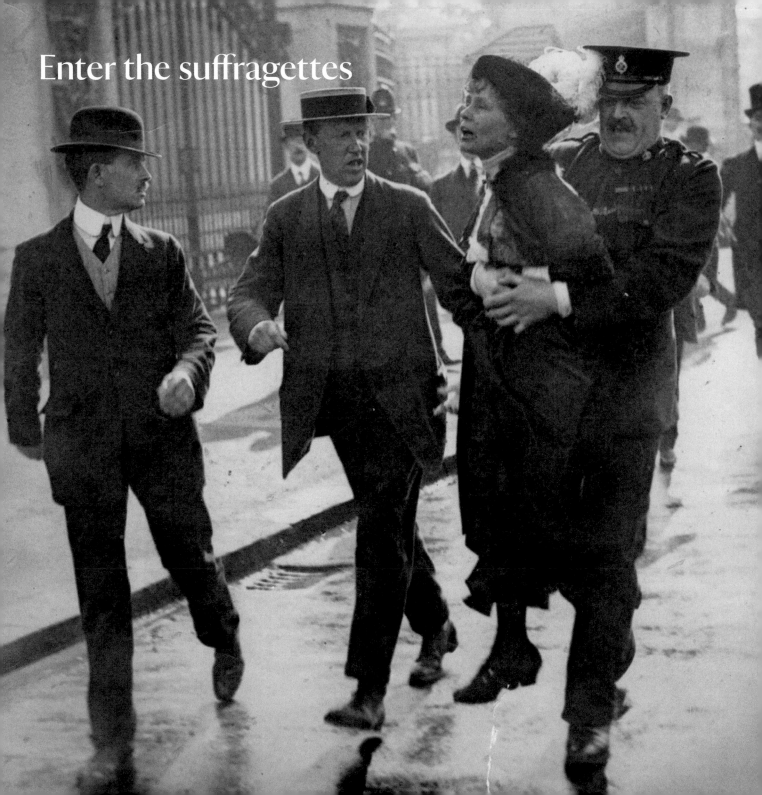

Enter the suffragettes

The suffragettes were instantly controversial. George Bernard Shaw, asked for his opinion in 1906, provocatively replied that suffragettes 'should shoot, maim, kill, destroy'. For some women, conversion to the suffrage cause was visceral and immediate. Evelyn Sharp's life was transformed by a single speech from suffragette actress Elizabeth Robins, but her worried mother made her promise not to do anything to get herself arrested.

In 1911, her mind changed, Evelyn's mother released her from the promise: 'I am writing to exonerate you from the promise you made me – as regards being arrested – although I hope you will never go to prison, still I feel I cannot any longer be so prejudiced and must really leave it to your own better judgment. [...] I cannot write more but you will be happy now, won't you?' Within a year, Sharp was in Holloway for smashing government windows.

Other suffrage groups emerged. In 1907, the Women's Freedom League (WFL) formed, advocating non-violent protests such as refusing to pay tax until women got the vote. Evelyn Sharp was also a member of the Women Writers' Suffrage League (WWSL), followed by the Actresses' Franchise League (AFL) in 1908, whose founder members included Ellen Terry and Edith Craig. Although the most prominent part of the movement, the WSPU never had more than 2,000 members, while the WFL had 4,000 and the NUWSS peaked at 50,000 in 1913.

The NUWSS remained active throughout suffragette activism's early years. In fact, it was a 1908 NUWSS demonstration that inspired mother-and-daughter suffragettes Sybil Thomas and Margaret Mackworth, Lady Rhondda. Suffragist Sybil attended alongside her daughter, thinking it was unsuitable to let Margaret, aged 25, attend unchaperoned. Both later went to prison, Sybil for illegal meetings outside Parliament and Margaret for bombing a postbox.

Banners and more
Jessie Wylie Rowat, who lived in the Eastgate of **Corfe Castle**, was a suffragette embroiderer and designer who stitched suffrage banners. An active WSPU member, she also believed in 'Rational Dress': healthy, corset-free fashion that led to 'divided skirts' and the first women's trousers.

Opposite Emmeline Pankhurst is arrested and carried away outside of Buckingham Palace, May 1914. Pankhurst had organised a march to petition the King and was met with violence

Above This poster advertising *The Suffragette* newspaper features a suffragette dressed as Joan of Arc, patron saint of the cause. The 1912 image reflects the increasingly militant tone of the later stages of the campaign

Decentring men

By self-consciously forming a women's movement and caring for women who had been injured or imprisoned, suffragists were displacing men in an intensely patriarchal world. Some of these women were in same-sex relationships or gender non-conforming. But regardless of their sexuality, suffrage activists lived their lives in radical ways.

The diaries of suffragette Mary Blathwayt, related to the Blathwayts of **Dyrham Park**, reveal the network of intimate relationships between Annie Kenney, Christabel Pankhurst and others. Blathwayt was infatuated with Kenney, who gave her a brooch 'from Annie with Love'. Blathwayt's mother noted in a 1908 diary entry that WSPU activism and Annie Kenney made Mary 'intensely happy'.

Vera 'Jack' Holme was an actress employed by the D'Oyly Carte Company (owned by the D'Oyly Carte family of **Coleton Fishacre**), and later Edith Craig's Pioneer Players at **Smallhythe**. A member of the WSPU and AFL, Holme became chauffeur to the Pankhursts. Photographs reveal her masculine appearance. Her partner was the Hon. Evelina Haverfield, a fellow WSPU activist who spent time in prison for assaulting a police officer and disrupting demonstrations.

Annie Leigh Browne and her partner Mary Kilgour were activists and benefactors together in London and the South West. Leigh Browne became the driving force behind the Women's Local Government Society and the Women's Educational Union. In her will, she left **The Byes**, a two-mile stretch of parkland, meadowland and farmland near Sidmouth, to the National Trust.

Better-known than all of the above was Virginia Woolf, who was drawn into the NUWSS out of admiration for her former tutor, the classicist Janet Case. Woolf later had an affair with Vita Sackville-West. Both were lifelong friends of Edith Craig and Christopher St John, who remained a couple from 1899 until Craig's 1947 death, with artist Clare Atwood joining their partnership in 1916.

Chauvinist rebukes

Anti-suffragists such as Rudyard Kipling of **Bateman's** claimed that the *real* 'driving force' of suffrage activists was the desire to be near political men. In a letter, he argued that unmarried suffragettes 'consciously or unconsciously want a man and don't care a curse for the politics', while married activists were 'without power to hold or charm the man they've got'. Sexual slurs and assaults became increasingly common for activists, making the lives of women who expressed sexual or gender difference even more fraught.

Right Photograph of Vera 'Jack' Holme, chauffeur to the Pankhursts and the Women's Social and Political Union. She is dressed in her purple, white and green uniform

Far right A 'welcome' breakfast for suffragettes released from Holloway Prison, 1908

Celebrating success

Suffragettes celebrated each other's release from prison with breakfasts and banquets. One such, feting the release of Anne Cobden-Sanderson in October 1906, was hosted by NUWSS President Millicent Fawcett at London's Savoy Hotel, and brought together NUWSS suffragists with WSPU suffragettes and socialists like Charlotte Shaw.

1910

On 21 June 1910, pro- and anti-suffrage deputations visited Prime Minister Asquith in Downing Street. Laura McLaren represented the Liberal suffragists. Her rival, Lady Jersey, argued that: 'The opponents of woman suffrage did not think that women were more stupid than men, but they knew that their hands were overfull already.'

A month later Lady Jersey and Lord Curzon of **Kedleston**, Britain's leading male anti-suffragist, co-signed a *Times* letter fundraising for a National Anti-Suffrage League, describing themselves as 'unutterably opposed to the grant of woman suffrage', alongside bishops, academics and aristocrats.

In November 1910, the pro-suffrage 'Conciliation Bill' failed. A number of MPs resident in National Trust properties had tried to push this bill forward, including Hugh Luttrell at **Dunster Castle** and Noel Buxton at **Paycocke's**. The failure led to 'Black Friday',

Left Postcard designed by Harold Bird, to announce a meeting in the Royal Albert Hall, organised by the National League for Opposing Woman Suffrage. The feminine central figure politely refuses the vote whilst, behind her, a suffragette inelegantly leaps towards Parliament, brandishing a hammer

Above Suffragette Black Friday, 1910. Outside the Houses of Parliament a group, led by Emmeline Pankhurst, held a six-hour siege that ended with dozens of arrests and brutal assaults on women

when 300 suffragettes attempted to storm Parliament and were brutalised by police. Evelyn Sharp saw 'a hospital nurse' assaulted by 'four mounted men', while Sylvia Pankhurst witnessed women with 'broken noses, bruises, sprains, and dislocations'. Some reported sexual assault by police. Also present was Violet Ann Bland, a working-class suffragette who had formerly worked as a kitchenmaid at **Dudmaston Hall**. She was arrested, alongside 116 other women and two men, but the Home Secretary declined to prosecute.

Religion and the anti-suffragists

Religious arguments were crucial to many anti-suffragists' objections to women's enfranchisement. National Trust founder Octavia Hill had, from the outset of the suffrage movement, been cited by suffragists as an example of a public woman who clearly deserved the vote. Millicent Fawcett listed her alongside Jane Austen and Florence Nightingale in one 1886 speech. Yet, in her 1910 letter, Hill argued against suffrage. Rooted in religious belief, she described the voteless state as one 'to which by God's appointment [woman] is called'.

Lady Emily Acland, a relative of the **Killerton** Aclands, felt women should 'set up a high standard for ourselves of purity and devotion to God and duty', rather than chase the vote. She saw women's questioning of Christian marriage as an attack on the Empire.

Many leading anti-suffragists were active in the Church; the Dowager Duchess of Newcastle, Henrietta Adela Pelham-Clinton, was a Roman Catholic anti-suffragist who served as vice-president of the Association of Perpetual Adoration.

'The stability and happiness of the Empire rests eventually on the stability and happiness of each home in the Empire; and that again rests on one only sure foundation, the inviolability and sanctity of the marriage vow. But the sanctity of marriage is being called in question on all sides today.'

Lady Emily Acland

Radical religion

Conversely, many suffragists saw their religious beliefs as integral to their activism. Within the Church of England, the wives of two successive Bishops of Southwell, Laura Ridding and Mary Hoskyns, campaigned for suffrage, as well as women and children in poverty in **Southwell Workhouse**.

Ridding, a friend of fellow Liberal suffragists Millicent Fawcett, Eleanor Acland and Laura McLaren, co-founded the National Union of Women Workers, and encouraged her fellow members to support suffrage, saying their Union would better 'influenc[e] public opinion when it had the weight of votes behind it'. Mary Hoskyns, meanwhile, founded Southwell's branch of the NUWSS, having volunteered to do so at a 1910 meeting in Nottingham, saying she had been a suffragist 'for several years'. Both Laura and Mary were involved in the Church League for Women's Suffrage, founded in 1909.

Unitarians and Quakers

Appropriately, however, it was from two Nonconformist denominations that the real support for women's suffrage came. Unitarianism is a progressive, non-dogmatic belief system whose first British congregations emerged in the 1770s, rejecting the doctrine of the Trinity. After the movement was legalised in 1813, followers included authors Charles Dickens, Elizabeth Gaskell and Louisa May Alcott. The Victorian Unitarians had women ministers, and numerous leading suffragists were Unitarians. Agnes and Henry Pochin, who hosted the first ever public suffrage meeting in 1868, were Unitarians, as was their daughter Laura McLaren, the Trevelyans of **Wallington**, the Gregs and Dowsons of **Quarry Bank**, and Annie Leigh Browne.

The Society of Friends, known as the 'Quakers', also contributed. Both the Unitarians and the Quakers had fiercely opposed slavery in Britain and its Empire. Later, Dorothy Frances Jebb (connected to the Buxtons at **Paycocke's**) was a leading Quaker peace activist. Perhaps the most famous British Quaker ever, the prison reformer and women's advocate Elizabeth Fry, close friend of the **Peckover** family, became a role model for suffragettes. Her name appeared on suffrage banners, she was referenced in speeches, and commemorated in suffrage novels. Even Queen Victoria, who detested women's suffrage, was a great admirer of Fry. Today, both Quakers and Unitarians remain committed to sexual equality.

Far left Suffragist and campaigner Laura McLaren

Left Northcliffe Unitarian Chapel, which was attended by the Greg family at Quarry Bank

Right Quaker and reformer Elizabeth Fry, 1823

Elizth Fry.

Protest and prayer

Christian suffragists frequently interrupted church services to pray aloud for imprisoned activists. In October 1913, a Birmingham Cathedral service was suspended by 20 women chanting a prayer for 'all the Suffragist prisoners. Save them, save them, their enemies torture them; they are persecuted; they suffer for conscience sake.'

Force-feeding

Initially, imprisoned suffragettes who went on hunger strike were released when their health deteriorated, but in 1909 force-feeding began. Over 1,000 suffragette prisoners were force-fed, through the throat, nose and, in a few cases, the rectum.

Violet Ann Bland was a kitchenmaid at **Dudmaston** before joining the WSPU. After breaking windows in March 1912, she was sentenced to four months' imprisonment in Aylesbury prison, where she joined the hunger strike and was forcibly fed. Interviewed alongside Emmeline Pankhurst in *Votes for Women*, Bland recalled her experience:

'They pinched and clutched my nose unmercifully, and at the end of the assault, when I did not rise quickly from the chair because of my helpless and breathless condition, they snatched the chair from under me, and flung me on the floor [...] The whole of the work is done in the greatest rush and hurry. There is no doubt whatsoever about the attacks being made with the object of breaking us down [...] During the strike the wardresses were transformed into inhuman brutes and fiends, and one could not but feel that, like the police on Black Friday, they were being made use of by the Government for this dastardly purpose [...] My heart and circulation were in an alarming condition during these operations;

Right Suffragette being force-fed in Holloway Prison, 1909. Liquid is poured into a tube that has been forced up her nose. Many suffragettes suffered long-term health consequences from the trauma of hunger strikes and force-feeding

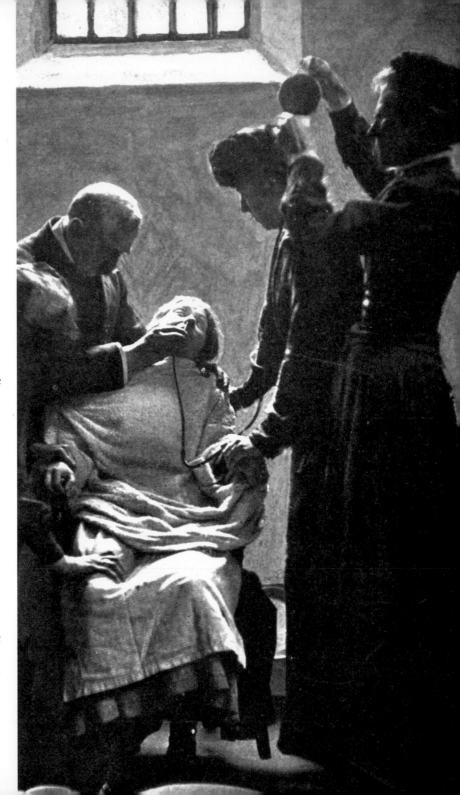

but never through either hunger strike was my pulse noted. On Wednesday, June 26, they twisted my neck, jerked my head back, closing my throat, held all the time as in a vice. I gasped for breath, and suffered tortures mentally lest the food which they were trying to pour down my throat should go into my lungs. They do not expect, or intend, one to swallow the food, but pour it into one's stomach as through an open water-pipe. They expect, and try, to perform the whole operation in two minutes. There were always six or seven to one, so that there was really no possibility of the victim doing much in the way of protesting, excepting verbally, to express one's horror of it.'

Cat and Mouse

Many activists likened force-feeding to rape. Working-class women were more likely to be brutalised than aristocratic activists: Lady Constance Bulwer-Lytton, related to the aristocratic Villiers family of **Upton House**, repeatedly escaped force-feeding until she deliberately went to Walton prison under the working-class alias 'Jane Warton'. The Prisoners' (Temporary Discharge for Ill Health) Act (1913) allowed for the release of prisoners made ill by hunger-striking and force-feeding, only for their sentences to recommence once they had recovered. Passed by the Liberal government, the Act was extremely unpopular, and known as the 'Cat and Mouse' Act for its cruelty.

Right This poster by 'A Patriot' depicts a very similar scene. It calls for an end to the torture of this 'modern inquisition' by voting against Prime Minister Herbert Asquith

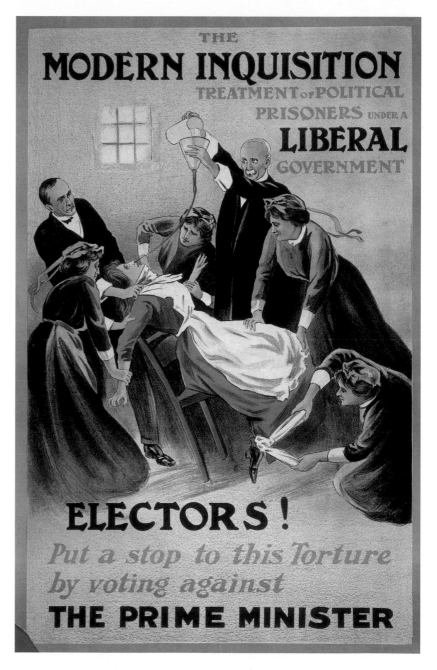

Death at the Derby

Born in Morpeth, Northumberland, Emily Wilding Davison was an intensely committed WSPU and workers' activist. Highly intelligent, she took First Class Honours in English at St Hugh's College, Oxford – but since women could not graduate, she received no degree.

Having joined the WSPU, she became an enthusiastic suffragette alongside women like Jessie Rowat of **Corfe Castle**, Lady Rhondda, Violet Ann Bland, Constance Bulwer-Lytton and Christopher St John of **Smallhythe**. In 1911, on the night of the census, she hid in a broom cupboard in the Houses of Parliament to have Britain's political epicentre recorded as her home.

After being sent to prison for stone-throwing, Davison was left traumatised by force-feeding in Strangeways Prison in Manchester. Having barricaded herself into her cell to avoid the assault, she attempted suicide as a 'desperate protest' against the 'hideous torture' she and her fellow prisoners had experienced. She came round in 'acute agony'. Later re-imprisonments (for arson, vandalism, and assault – not all authorised by the WSPU) and 49 bouts of force-feedings convinced her that the suffrage movement required a martyr.

The fateful day

On 4 June 1913, Davison attended the Derby. Mid-race, she ran out onto the course and tried to grab the bridle of Anmer, King George V's horse, possibly to attach a WSPU scarf. Mary Richardson, her fellow suffragette, described her as calm and smiling in the moments before she ran. The horse hit her; she was 'knocked over screaming' (*Daily Mirror*), stupefied, and died on 8 June, without regaining consciousness. The day before the Derby, she had lain a wreath before a statue of Joan of Arc, a religious icon for many suffragettes.

'Rebellion against tyrants is obedience to God.'

Emily Wilding Davison

Left Photograph of Emily Wilding Davison wearing a suffragette 'prisoner's brooch'

Above View of the Epsom Derby as Davison lies under King George V's horse, 4 June 1913

Right Davison's death, four days after the Derby, led to a huge funeral procession. Supporters carry a banner proclaiming, 'Fight on and God will give the victory'

The movement had its martyr. Davison's funeral was attended by thousands of women in WSPU colours, as well as trade unionists, academics and workers. Her body was returned to Morpeth by special train.

The press condemned Davison as mentally ill; *The Times* noted her 'inanity' and 'wickedness'. Yet, in the eyes of suffragist Alice Dowson, daughter of the Gregs of **Quarry Bank**: 'She *was* a heroine! having gone thro many imprisonments & forcible feeding, yet people don't seem to see it & say such horrid things about her'. Anmer ended his days on a Canada stud farm. His jockey, Herbert Jones, was traumatised by 'that poor woman's face'; he laid a wreath to her and Emmeline Pankhurst at the latter's 1928 funeral, and died by suicide in 1951. Then and now, there remains some doubt Davison meant to kill herself: she had purchased a return train ticket, and had left no message for her mother.

Were the suffragettes terrorists?

Between 1912 and 1914, suffragette violence intensified to include arson and bombings. While activists were undoubtedly accused of crimes they probably did not commit – such as the 1914 fire at Clevedon Court's parish church – escalating instances of proven arson attacks, assaults on politicians, and bombs have led some historians to argue that the suffragettes were terrorists.

In Dublin in July 1912, Mary Leigh, a WSPU activist, hurled a hatchet at Asquith in what can only be seen as an assassination attempt. Hours later, Leigh, Gladys Evans and associates set fire to a projector and planted a bomb in the crowded Theatre Royal. One Glasgow suffragette fired a gun (loaded with blanks) at police arresting Emmeline Pankhurst. Twelve builders almost died when suffragettes planted nail bombs in a cottage belonging to politician David Lloyd George. Artworks including the Rokeby Venus by Velázquez and a portrait of author Henry James were slashed, and the coronation chair in Westminster Abbey was damaged by another bomb. Across Britain, explosives were planted in railways, bridges, libraries and churches. These attacks fit the definition of terrorism under the 2000 Terrorism Act: politically motivated violence designed to damage property, endanger public health and safety and, on occasion, threaten individuals' lives.

Right Suffragette in purple, green and white threatens men with a smoking bomb and hammer

"MEN ARE NOT ALL ANGELS, BUT SOME SOON WILL BE!"

Occasionally, suffragettes left warnings – a bomb placed outside Newcastle Assize in April 1913 was labelled 'run for your life'. Although the only confirmed deaths resulting from proven suffrage action were those of suffragettes themselves, this was more luck than judgement. One bomb in particular, tied to railings outside the Bank of England in 1913, opposite the Stock Exchange, might have killed hundreds had a police constable not disabled it. Between April 1913 and the outbreak of the First World War, suffragette bomb technology improved: explosives contained nitroglycerine, and letter bombs were sent to politicians and magistrates. Lady Rhondda is usually described as having 'set fire' to a postbox in 1913. In fact, she pushed a bomb inside, consisting of an 'explosive substance' in two glass tubes, one of which contained phosphorous and the other 'a chemical compound, the nature of which was only disclosed to the Bench'. Other devices detonated near Holloway Prison shattered the windows of nearby houses, covering sleeping residents – including children – in broken glass.

Rebellion as obligation
The Pankhursts told their WSPU followers that militancy was a moral duty; Emmeline Pankhurst justified the attack on Lloyd George's house in Surrey on the basis that Britain was in a state of 'insurrection'. Without the outbreak of the First World War, the escalating violence almost certainly would have led to civilian deaths.

Top The tea pavillion at Kew Gardens, burnt down by suffragette Olive Wharry

Right The burnt-out shell of Saunderton station, Buckinghamshire, destroyed by suffragettes in March 1913

War and Victory 1914–1918

THESE WOMEN ARE DOING THEIR BIT

LEARN TO MAKE MUNITIONS

Once Britain declared war on Germany on 4 August 1914, the NUWSS and WSPU suspended suffrage campaigning for war work, in exchange for the release of suffragette prisoners.

Many activists became passionately pro-war. Emmeline and Christabel Pankhurst spoke at recruitment drives, and Christabel undertook an American and Canadian speaking tour in which she blamed Germany's aggression on its being a 'masculine' nation. Meanwhile, NUWSS leader Millicent Fawcett avowed in 1915 that: 'I believe it is akin to treason to talk of peace.'

Pacifists
These attitudes were divisive. Pacifist Sylvia Pankhurst objected that women would 'bear the harder part of the suffering [… as] the men-made Governments of Europe rush heedless on to war.' Disgusted at Fawcett's jingoism, suffragist Catherine Marshall (who campaigned in **Borrowdale and Derwentwater**) resigned from the NUWSS, becoming secretary of the No-Conscription Fellowship. Dorothy Jebb, sister-in-law to MP Noel Buxton, was another suffragist pacifist, a Quaker who fought jingoism by publishing evidence of German anti-war demonstrations and suffering. Jebb later founded 'Save the Children'. The Women's Freedom League remained pacifist throughout the war, with member Edith Craig's Pioneer Players producing theatre that criticised the war.

Left **A patriotic poster encourages women to volunteer to aid the war effort**

Right (above) **Women working in a factory**

Right (below) **Women barrowing coke at a gas works, 1916**

Women's war effort

The numbers of British women in the workforce rose dramatically, from 3.25 million in July 1914 to 4.8 million by January 1918. About 200,000 women worked in government departments and 700,000 (mainly working class) in dangerous munitions roles. Edith Vane-Tempest-Stewart became colonel-in-chief of the Women's Volunteer Reserve, while Lady Rhondda became commissioner of women's National Service for Wales. Vera 'Jack' Holme became a Major in the Women's Volunteer Reserve, travelling to Serbia to report on the humanitarian crisis. Aristocrats including Nancy Astor transformed their homes into military hospitals. Women's wartime service impressed some men, but benefitted working women too.

Princesses at work

Princess Sudhira Mander, of Cooch Behar in west Bengal, married into the fiercely pro-suffrage Mander family of **Wightwick** in February 1914. Known for her style and overspending, Sudhira also agitated for Anglo-Indian relations and fundraised for Indian Allied soldiers, alongside Princess Sophia Duleep Singh, Queen Victoria's goddaughter, supposedly the 'only' British Asian suffragette. Sophia and Sudhira joined the Red Cross on the outbreak of war, learning nursing and first aid, and were honoured at the same 1915 Red Cross ceremony. In 1917, Sudhira helped Sophia organise the Indian section of 'Our Day', a huge Red Cross fundraising event. Their section – devoted to injured Indian soldiers – encompassed key London locations, including the Haymarket and St James's Square.

'The war, awful as it has been, has been a wonderful thing for women. […] they have learned to have confidence in themselves to undertake the most amazing and difficult tasks.'

Lady Rhondda

AT LAST!

Anti-suffrage activism in wartime

Although the war converted many men to the suffrage cause, the core group of anti-suffragists – including Lord Curzon, Lady Jersey and Rudyard Kipling – remained vehemently opposed. In November 1916, they co-authored a letter to *The Times*, asserting that a wartime Parliament had 'no moral right' to extend suffrage, and were 'unable to admit that recent circumstances' i.e. women's war work 'justifi[ed] any serious modification of the conclusions at which they have previously arrived'. They vowed 'to offer, by all legitimate means, the most strenuous opposition to the extension of electoral rights to women'.

The Speaker's Conference

In early 1916, rumours reached the suffragists that the government was considering legislation to enfranchise all soldiers serving overseas, as a reward for serving their country. Millicent Fawcett immediately wrote to Asquith highlighting women's own 'active, self-sacrificing and efficient national service'. The newly created Consultative Committee of Women's Suffrage Societies argued in August 1916 that if the franchise were 'established based on services in the war then the claim of women […] cannot be ignored.'

In October 1916, a cross-party body called the Speaker's Conference met to consider whether to enfranchise women and working-class men. A month later a group of suffragists including Eleanor Acland, Lady Laura Ridding, Millicent Fawcett, Annie Leigh Browne and socialist Beatrice Webb wrote to *The Times*. They argued that the 'changed position of women in industry' and the fact that the war had made women 'heads of wholly unrepresented households' made it 'essential that women themselves should be heard' in deciding their – and Britain's – political future. Eleanor's husband, Liberal MP Francis Dyke Acland, was optimistic about the results of the conference, writing to her in

January that 'if anything is done at all women must get the vote unless we suffs play the utter ass.' He was right.

Why did some women get the vote?

The Representation of the People Act (January 1918) enfranchised men over 21 and women over 30 who met certain property qualifications. Today, many believe that the exchange of militancy for war work won suffrage for women. In fact, the Act failed to enfranchise the working-class women who'd taken the most dangerous factory jobs.

Some politicians wanted to avoid a return to militant activism once the war had finished; the Liberal government was aware that continuing to oppose suffrage could mean losing votes to Labour, who were campaigning for 'Votes for All'.

Finally, the anti-suffrage Asquith had left office, replaced by the more suffrage-positive David Lloyd George. The WSPU, now renamed 'The Women's Party', saw the 'Great Suffrage Victory' as a spur for yet more patriotic war work, while for Evelyn Sharp, at least, it was 'almost the happiest night of my life'.

Left *Punch* cartoon, 'At Last!', marks women's right to vote, 1918

Below Women voting for the first time, 1918

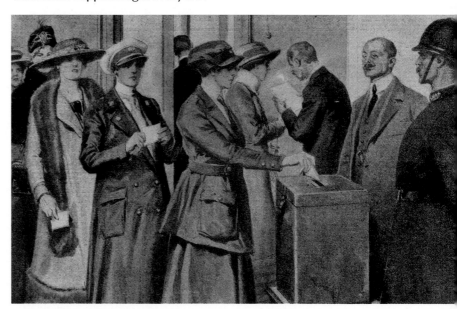

Post-War 1918–1928

It was 10 years after women first achieved the Parliamentary vote that the battle for equal franchise was won. Between 1918 and 1928 suffragist women and men continued the struggle across a decade of profound social and political change.

Members of Parliament

The first woman to be elected to Parliament was Constance Markievicz in 1918. It is a strong reminder of the complexity and many-sided nature of women's activism that, as a Sinn Fein representative, she did not take her seat.

The first woman to sit in the House of Commons was Nancy Astor, of **Cliveden**. When her husband entered the House of Lords in 1919, she stood for his seat, Plymouth Sutton, and held it until 1945. In Astor we see the journey from political wife, exercising power through what Edith Vane-Tempest-Stewart called 'apologetic' influence, to active and established politician at the centre of formal British power.

'I know that it was very difficult for some hon. Members to receive the first lady MP into the House,' she said in her maiden speech in the House of Commons on 24 February 1920. 'It was almost as difficult for some of them as it was for the lady MP herself to come in.'

Left Nancy Astor is proclaimed Member of Parliament in a 1919 by-election

Opposite (left) The Astor family on the terrace of their palatial home at Cliveden, December 1921

Opposite (right) Astor's victory is featured on the front page of the *New Illustrated*, 15 November 1919

Before her election, Nancy Astor had not been an active suffragist, though by 1924 she was regarded in the Press as 'an out-and-out champion for the extension of the suffrage'. The Cliveden guestbook shows that ardent suffrage campaigners George Bernard Shaw and Sylvia Pankhurst later stayed as guests.

The Astors' phenomenal wealth is evident to all visitors to Cliveden today and Nancy's fitness to represent her constituents was questioned in the press: 'We believe that ground rents are or were a burning question in Plymouth. What is the source of the Astor fortune? Unless we are mistaken, their enormous income is derived from ground rents in New York, which has as many slums as London.'

Astor spent almost two years as the only woman in the House of Commons and, like so many women who break into male-dominated professions, she encountered entrenched sexism and open resentment. Many MPs refused to speak to her. Winston Churchill later told her 'we hoped to freeze you out'. In the 2017 general election more women were elected to the House of Commons than ever before: 32% of the Parliamentary representatives of Britain.

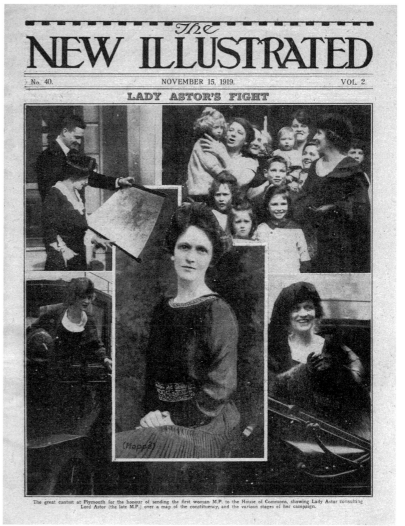

The NEW ILLUSTRATED

No. 40. NOVEMBER 15, 1919. VOL. 2.

LADY ASTOR'S FIGHT

(Hoppé)

The great contest at Plymouth for the honour of sending the first woman M.P. to the House of Commons, showing Lady Astor consulting Lord Astor (the late M.P.) over a map of the constituency, and the various stages of her campaign.

'I had the privilege of being the first woman in the House of Commons, and sometimes I used to doubt whether it was a privilege. When I stood up and asked questions affecting women and children, social and moral questions, I used to be shouted at for 5 or 10 minutes at a time. That was when they thought that I was rather a freak, a voice crying in the wilderness.'

Nancy Astor in 1928 reflecting on her early days in the House of Commons

The 'last' demonstration

The campaigns pursued by suffragists and suffragettes diversified in the 1920s. In 1921, Viscountess Rhondda formed a Six Point Group whose 'points' demanded legislation on child assault, widowed mothers, single mothers and their children, equal parental rights, equal pay for teachers, and equality of opportunity for men and women in the civil service. Rhondda argued that the right to vote must be the beginning of a wave of social and economic reform.

Yet, even as attention shifted and suffragist groups rebranded or disbanded, the Representation of the People Act remained a partial victory. Though the absolute exclusion of women from the parliamentary franchise had been overcome, the equal right of women to participate in the political sphere had been by no means asserted in the 1918 Act. Fears over women becoming the majority of the electorate following the First World War, as well as an entrenched belief in the relative incapacity of women, were pacified by the exclusion of the youngest and poorest. Half a generation was disempowered in this newly expressed inequality.

Eight years after first achieving the vote, Viscountess Rhondda would find herself again speaking for equal franchise in a Hyde Park demonstration. She spoke alongside Emmeline Pankhurst, Millicent Fawcett and Emmeline Pethick-Lawrence expressing a shared desire for this to be the last protest. In 1927, the following year, she chaired a platform at a Trafalgar Square rally at which one of the square's stone lions sported a placard declaring: 'Gentlemen prefer blondes, but blondes prefer the vote.'

The 1926 Hyde Park demonstration would prove not to be the last to demand equal franchise and was far from the last demonstration for gender equality. In 2017, 90 years after Viscountess Rhondda took over Trafalgar Square, 100,000 people again rallied to this landmark in an international Women's March to promote equality in response to a rise in public misogyny. Some protesters arrived dressed as suffragettes; others brought placards with slogans that read: 'I can't believe I still have to protest this shit.'

'All these women organisations want this to be the last Procession and Demonstration to demand equal franchise. There is much important work waiting to be done in connection with Education, Child Welfare and Housing, Equal Pay and Equal Opportunities, but before concentrating on these questions it is necessary for women to obtain the political power which will enable them to secure the reforms they wish to see. The first thing, therefore, is to win political equality.'

The Woman Teacher, 1926

Left Demonstration for the equal
franchise for men and women in
London, 1926

Above Protesters march in London to
promote women's equal rights in the
wake of the US election result, 2017

The Equal Franchise Act

The 1918 Representation of the People Act marked a shift in public opinion that pointed the way towards full reform. By the time the Conservative government passed equal franchise in 1928, it was with relatively limited controversy. The 1918 Act had broken the ground and a perception of the arbitrariness of the disparity had begun to show across the political spectrum – something that the nation would experience again in 2013 when same-sex marriage was introduced nine years after the Civil Partnership Act had set the precedent.

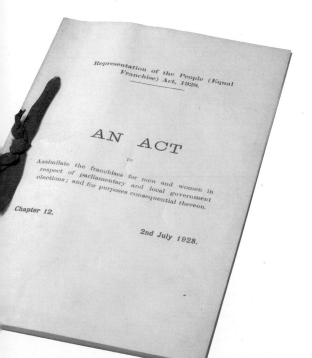

In June the Bill was passed in the House of Lords – 'by sad coincidence' on the day of Emmeline Pankhurst's funeral. Lady Rhondda's feminist, left-wing culture magazine *Time and Tide* marked the occasion: 'We of today stand much too close to the great changes for which Mrs Pankhurst was so largely responsible to be able to appreciate their immensity. It was not merely the achievement of the vote that the movement of which she was the leader brought about – it was far more than this, a revolution (or at least the beginning of a revolution, for the end is not yet) in the status of women and in their attitude towards themselves.'

In this year of victory for equal suffrage, Virginia Woolf observed that the history of opposition to women's emancipation was 'more interesting perhaps than the story of that emancipation itself.' We have found many inspiring stories of women and men who fought for women's right to vote across National Trust places and collections. One of the most consistent features that we see in these varied and personal struggles is the entrenched and vicious opposition faced by these champions. As she looked back on the struggle for 'women's emancipation', Woolf challenged us to remember both sides of this debate; she warned us against complacency and compelled us to reflect on which side of that struggle history will find us.

Above Dame Millicent Fawcett, Miss Fawcett, Miss Garrett and Mrs Strachey celebrate Royal Assent to the Equal Franchise Act, 1928

Left Representation of the People (Equal Franchise) Act, 1928

Right The funeral of
Emmeline Pankhurst,
St John's Church, Smith
Square, London,
15 June 1928

'If any person had prophesied two years
ago, or even a year ago, that equal
political rights between men and
women could be universally accepted
within so short a period, that it would be
possible today for an Equal Franchise Bill
to pass its Third Reading in the House of
Commons without division and even
without comment, a soul would hardly
have believed him [sic].'

Time and Tide, 11 May 1928

Epilogue

As we celebrate 100 years of women's votes in Britain, we remember how far we still have to go: that gender equality remains elusive and that the persecution of women and girls is entrenched in laws around the world today.

The fight has changed significantly since the struggle for suffrage and yet, when we look back at this history, it can feel uncomfortably familiar. In Victorian Britain, opponents of equality were already dismissing women's rights campaigners as redundant. For Winston Churchill, there was simply 'no necessity' and an 1889 petition claimed that 'during the past half century all the principal injustices of the law towards women have been amended.' The gendered language used to disarm activists continues to draw from the stereotypes given to the 'unsexed' feminists and suffragists of this period.

Men and women continue to fight on both sides of contemporary debates about gender equality and the most established movements remain disproportionately white and relatively privileged. Both a century ago and today, the most vulnerable and poorest women and girls, and those who express gender nonconformity, are the people we see left furthest behind.

As we reflect on the lives of the women, and men, who achieved equal franchise it is impossible to quantify the work, time and energy that was sacrificed to overcome those who opposed women's presence at the ballot box. The struggle to achieve the extension of the franchise was characterised by debate around the legitimacy of a woman's voice and whether women have the right to fight for public rights at all.

Emmeline Pankhurst stated the desire of suffragists and suffragettes to move beyond the fight for their right to vote: to be 'law makers' not 'law breakers'. They fought for women to have a voice, a public role, to ensure that their views on the world had a chance to be heard and to give the women who came after them the opportunity to enact the change we want to see in the world today.

The challenge of this century will be to ensure that this legacy is inherited by all; both to imagine and to demand equality in a world where, still, as Pankhurst saw, 'justice and judgement lie often a world apart.' In 2013, in a speech to the United Nations, Malala Yousafzai perhaps said it best when she reflected simply: 'We cannot all succeed when half of us are held back.'

Left Emmeline
Pankhurst, c.1910

Right Nobel Peace
Prize winner Malala
Yousafzai, 2016

Women and Power in 2018

'We were the people who were not in the papers. We lived in the blank white spaces at the edges of print. It gave us more freedom. We lived in the gaps between the stories.'

Margaret Atwood, *The Handmaid's Tale*

The National Trust's Women and Power programme shines light on the extraordinary and ordinary women who lived and worked across England, Wales and Northern Ireland.

A century after women first achieved the vote, we are looking beyond the struggle for suffrage to give voice to some of the many women who went before. Women's lives inevitably run throughout all the places and collections of the National Trust. Some were the homes and creations of women who stand out in history – Bess of Hardwick, who amassed huge personal power in the reign of Elizabeth I; sexually liberated Vita Sackville-West of Sissinghurst; and Beatrix Potter, artist, businesswoman and Lake District conservationist. Many other less celebrated women sat behind the facades of mills, mansions, gardens and cottages. They are often harder to find and to draw out as clearly as their male kin or elite sisters; less frequently represented in art and archives.

The people we commemorate provide the markers of our history and serve as inspiration for new generations. In 2018, a statue of Millicent Fawcett is to be unveiled in Parliament Square, the first woman to stand at this seat of national power. In the campaign to see this extraordinary suffragist memorialised, research found that only

Left Vita Sackville-West at Sissinghurst, *c*.1950

2.5% of public statues in the United Kingdom are of historical women who weren't members of the royal family.

The histories of women often come to us through the blank spaces at the edges of print, in the gaps between the stories we were taught in school. The Challenging Histories programme of the National Trust aims to change that.

In 2018, Women and Power will feature new exhibitions, events, research, artist commissions and podcasts. The voices of women and girls who lived and worked in National Trust places will speak louder than ever before. They will echo through the stories we share for years, and generations, to come.